First published 2000 AD
This edition © Wooden Books 2001 AD

Published by Wooden Books Ltd.
Walkmill, Cascob, Presteigne, Powys, Wales LD8 2NT

British Library Cataloguing in Publication Data
Francis, E.
Avebury

A CIP catalogue record for this important book
is available from the British Library

ISBN 1 902418 23 9

Printed and bound in Great Britain
by The Cromwell Press,
Trowbridge, Wiltshire, UK.

AVEBURY

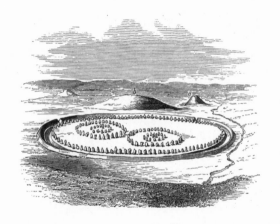

by

Evelyn Francis

Dedicated to the kind curators of the Alexander Keiller museum.

Do read "Prehistoric Avebury" by Aubrey Burl, "Avebury" by Caroline Malone and "Legendary Landscapes" by John & Julie Wakefield.

Pictures have mainly been taken from William Stukeley's book "Abury, a Temple of the British Druids", 1743, and from "Ancient Wiltshire" by Sir Richard Colt Hoare, 1819. The illustration on the cover is from "Rude Stone Monuments" by James Fergusson, 1872.

Many thanks to the Local Studies Unit, Wiltshire Library in Trowbridge for their help with the picture research for this book, and very particular thanks to Caius Hawkins.

INTRODUCTION

I have been visiting the great circles of Avebury since I was small and it is always with high heart and happy step that I approach the place. I have spent days there, nights there, even weeks there.

In this small book I have selected some of the more prominent features of the ancient sacred landscape which is Avebury – the Stones, Silbury Hill, the Sanctuary, the Avenue, the barrows, West Kennet Longbarrow, the Dolmen and, of course, the Spring. Each of these have their own special place around Avebury. The lost valleys, witchy woods and fairy dingles I will have to leave to the fleet of foot and keen of ear.

The diagrams used in the book are mostly from William Stukeley's book of 1743. I feel they convey the beauty and grandeur of the place better than modern pictures. Avebury Stone Circle now has a busy tarmacadam road through its centre and constant traffic deafens visitors.

The houses in the circle all now carry electric circuits and by night televisions flicker inside this ancient place. This is all a far cry from heavenly harmonies, horses, and hard work.

I have seen and experienced many strange things around Avebury, and have no doubt that the place was built for an other people in an other time and an other kind of mind and perception, now mostly lost.

I am indebted to Robin Heath for his kind assistance with the astronomy and geometry of Avebury, and to John Michell for other observations, thankyou also to Matthew Tweed for his illustration on page 31.

Avebury is a World Heritage Site; maybe one day the road will once again be grassed over and the circles again given some peace. That would be a powerful symbol for our time.

Wiltshire 2000

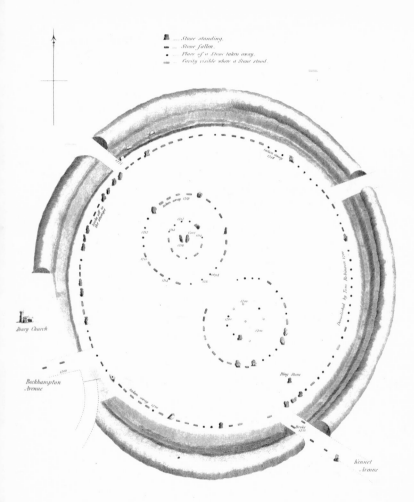

Stone standing.
Stone fallen.
Place of a Stone taken away.
Cavity visible where a Stone stood.

Abury Church

Beckhampton
Avenue

Kennet
Avenue

Bing Stone

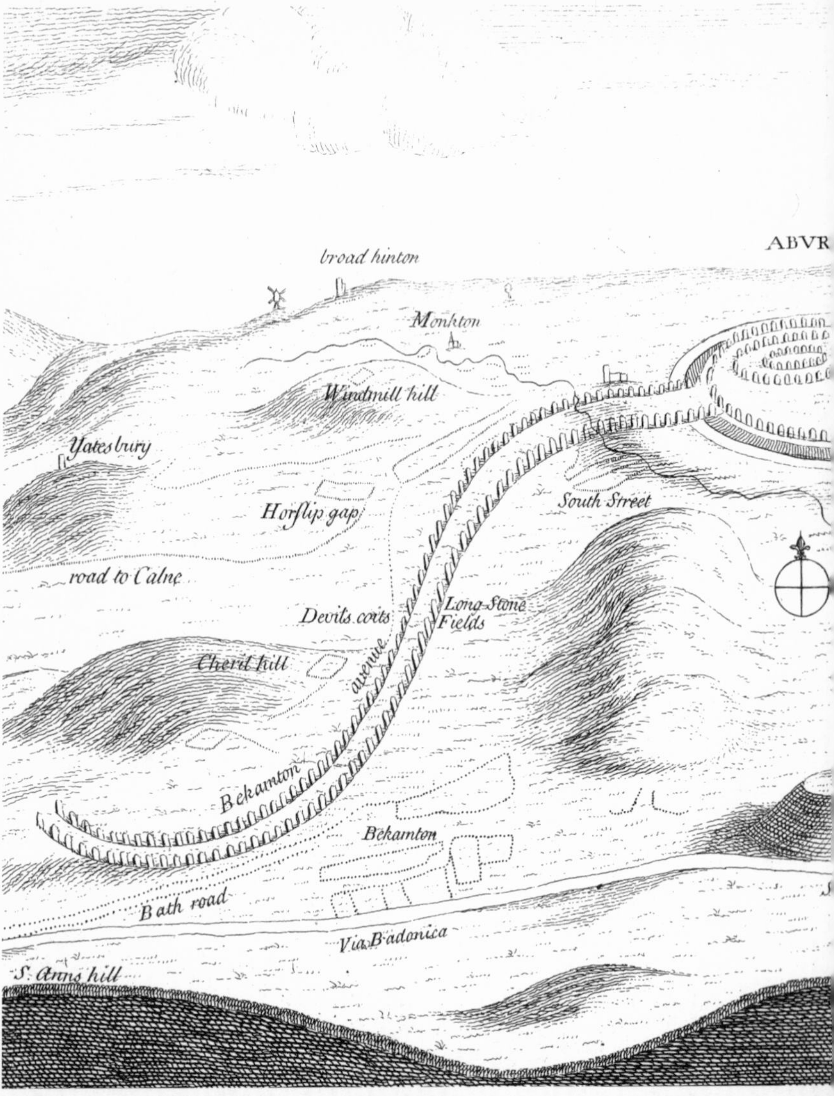

broad hinton

Monkton

Windmill hill

Yatesbury

Horslip gap

South Street

road to Calne

Devils coits

Long-Stone Fields

Cheril hill

avenue

Bekamton

Bekamton

Bath road

Via B'adonica

S.t Anns hill

Temple downs

The

Hakpen

hill

Windmill
hill

Kennet avenue

Overton hill

Kennetspring

Kennet river

S.Long barrow

Wansdike

West

THE CENTRE OF THE ISLE
Avebury as the centre of the 'Michael' line

If you draw a line from the western tip of our island to the eastern point then you will discover that Avebury is near the centre of that line. The line (known as the 'Michael line') passes through a number of ancient sacred sites, St. Michael's Mount, for instance, and the Hurlers Stone Circles. The two longest abbeys ever built on the island, at Glastonbury and Bury St. Edmunds, both lie on it. The ancient Ridgeway path and the Icknield Way also form parts of the line. The line marks the sunrise for Beltane (May Day) and Lammas, and the sunset for Imbolc and Samhain. These four special days lie halfway between the Solstices and the Equinoxes, the days of extremes and balancing. Thus if you watch the sunrise from Glastonbury Tor on May Day, it will rise over Avebury.

Avebury is also precisely at the centre of the three great watersheds of southern England. Water drains away from Avebury in every direction to the sea.

The Isle of Man is the ancient centre of the whole of the British Isles, circles centred there do interesting things.

AROUND AVEBURY

other ancient sites within easy walking distance

A short walk due north of Avebury (off the old map opposite) takes you up to the ancient settlement of Windmill Hill, occupied eight thousand years ago. There are huge barrows here which overlook the stone circles.

South of Avebury lies Silbury Hill, Swallowhead Spring and the West Kennet Longbarrow.

Running north-east along the ridge of Hackpen Hill is the long ancient track known as The Ridgeway. It runs from the ancient springs and Yew tree at Alton Priors, across another path, the Wansdyke, on top of the chalk downs near St. Anne's Hill, past the Sanctuary, Avebury and then off to Barbary Castle and other hill-forts far beyond in the direction of the May Day line (*see page 17*).

Walking east out of Avebury up the track to the Ridgeway gives easy access to the ancient and magical Fyfield Down, with its great sarsen stones, the source of the stones for both Avebury and Stonehenge.

West of Avebury can be found two large stones, called Adam and Eve, all that remain of a second avenue, and other barrows and long barrows all of which reward a visit.

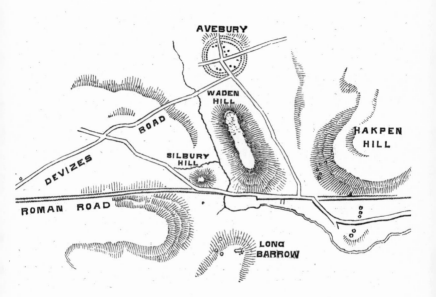

LOCKERIDGE

stones remain

When visiting Avebury it is a good idea to take one's time and wander widely in the area. In this way you may occasionally stumble across a lost stone or a forgotten but important barrow, and you will experience changing views and sensations which will all enrich your subtle understanding of the powerful and sacred landscape in which Avebury sits.

To get an idea of the nature of the landscape in slightly more ancient times, try visiting the small village of Lockeridge (*opposite below*), south of Avebury, where huge sarsen stones still lie where they fell when the ice melted twelve thousand years ago. Fyfield Down, to the east of Avebury is also well worth a visit for the same reason.

It could be argued that the best way to really get a feel for Avebury these days is to spend as little time there as possible, as it is badly affected by the lorries and the electrical circuits of the houses. There are even public toilets right in the middle of this once central and sacred place.

Viewing the henge from afar is therefore a must; it is good for the legs and can often be very rewarding.

11

THE BECKHAMPTON POT
evidence of fine craftmanship 5000 years ago

The pot shown opposite was found at Beckhampton near Avebury in the nineteenth century and is illustrated in Richard Colt-Hoare's book. It is a fine example of flat-bottomed grooveware. Earlier pots found in the area date from the early neolithic and mostly have rounded bottoms.

Later pots such as the ones shown here were often used as funery urns, containing the ashes of cremated individuals. Many have been found in burial chambers and barrows around Avebury by generations of grave-robbers and archaeologists. Other examples are shown below.

13

AUBREY'S AVEBURY
the first known sketch of the site

The first proper reference to Avebury appears in the 1610 edition of William Camden's *Britannia*, where he says:

> "Within one mile of Silbury is Abury ... it is environed with a fair trench, and hath four gates, in two of which stand huge stones as jambs ..."

Then in 1663 Charles II overheard the antiquarian John Aubrey mentioning that Avebury:

> "... did as much excell Stonehenge as a cathedral does a parish church".

The King was fascinated and visited the stones with Aubrey. Aubrey's plan of Avebury is shown opposite, the earliest known. Then, in 1743, William Stukeley produced the first good book on the site. He writes:

> "When we contemplate the elegance of this country of Wiltshire, and the great works of antiquity therein, we may be persuaded that the two atlantic islands, and the islands of the blessed, which Plato and other ancient writers mention, were those in reality of Britain and Ireland. They who first took possession of this country thought it worthy of their care, and built those noble works therein, which have been the admiration of all ages."

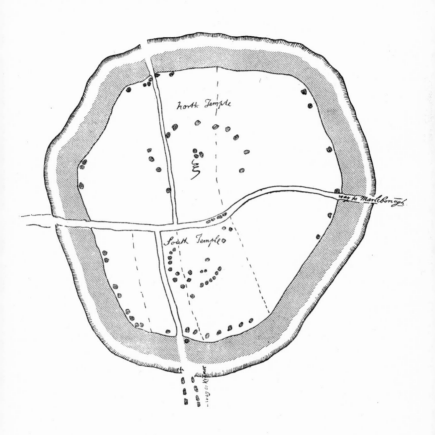

north Temple

South Temple

way to Marlborough

15

A MIGHTY TEMPLE
William Stukeley's wonderful vision

Although over three hundred years old, the engraving of the whole of Avebury (*pages 4-5 and detail opposite*) shows some of the key places in the Avebury landscape which can still be explored today .

The Stone Circles and the Avenue remain, just, and so does Silbury Hill. The Sanctuary on Overton Hill can still be visited and the West Kennet longbarrow. The Ridgeway can clearly be seen as a ridge in the right of the picture.

The Avebury complex was interpreted by William Stukeley as a Serpent Temple with the Sanctuary as the serpent's head. Archaeologists only recently found the westward avenue as they uncovered long-lost previously hidden stone-holes.

After living on Windmill Hill for a few thousand years, the people here then built Silbury Hill, about five thousand years ago, then the circles, the earthworks and finally the avenue. Some of them went south, dragging the massive sarsen stones from Fyfield Down and Lockeridge, the huge trilithon uprights which still stand at Stonehenge today.

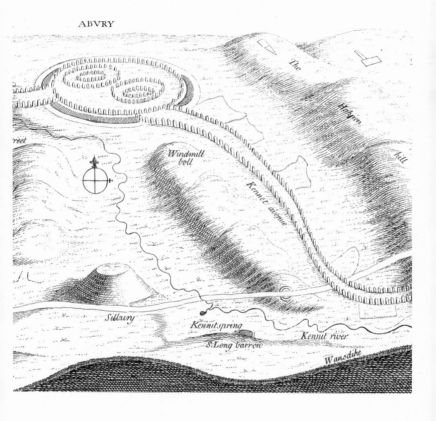

ABVRY

Street

Windmill hill

The Hagren hill

Kennet avenue

Sillury

Kennit spring

S. Long barron

Kennit river

Wansdike

17

THE SOUTH CIRCLE
what was left of it in Stukeley's day

As we have seen, there are two huge stone circles at Avebury *inside* the main outer 'Great' Circle. The part of the south circle still visible today is shown opposite, it is the circle which you see first on arriving in Avebury down the Avenue. As at Stonehenge the sarsens were dressed on the faces inside the circle, and left rough on their outer faces.

The South Circle consisted of 29 stones (*we will attempt to explain why on page 30*). At its centre stood a massive single stone, called the Obelisk (*see page 22*).

Visible in the engraving are three huge entrance stones (two now remain) and the *Ring Stone* between the outer circle and the south circle. Its stump is still there today.

There is evidence that the builders of Avebury attempted a third circle to the north of the other two but then gave up and dug the ditch instead. Sites with more than one stone circle are very rare in Britain. At Stanton Drew, a day's walk away, there are three stone circles, an avenue and a cove. Another beautiful site is the Hurlers (*see page 7*) where there are also three stone circles, one with 29 stones.

THE SOUTH ENTRANCE
the approach from the avenue

Avebury has four entrances – north, south, east and west. At each of these places the ditch is bridged and the henge has a gap.

The south entrance is the most spectacular today and must always have been important as the remaining avenue leads towards it. Two of the largest surviving stones mark the entrance place and as you approach down the Avenue, these two giant guardians of Avebury's great Outer Circle are hidden from you until the last moment.

The left-hand entrance stone, from outside the Circle has a place to sit in, and in a rainstorm will give you a shower from a hole above the seat. The gateway between the two entrance stones is thought to be very special as powerful 'ley' lines are said to cross there.

In Stukeley's day there were more stones than now as can be seen from the engraving. Avebury was being demolished as he studied it and almost all the stones we see today were put up again in the 1930's by Alexander Keiller, whose splendid museum lies adjacent to Avebury Church.

Abury

THE OBELISK

at the centre of the south circle

At the centre of the South Circle a huge stone known as the Obelisk once used to stand. It is shown fallen in Stukeley's picture. Twenty-nine stones originally surrounded the Obelisk, set at precisely the same average spacing as the outer circle, one every 36 feet, not an easy thing to do. Twenty nine plus the central one makes thirty, the same number of stones as the huge sarsen circle at Stonehenge. The South Circle was 340 feet across.

Near to the Obelisk, whose position is nowadays given by a curious cross-shaped concrete marker, stand a row of small stones. These are very peculiar and no-one has really explained them yet. They do, however, serve as an excellent shield from the road should you wish to sit quietly in the middle of this ancient place.

Perhaps the Obelisk was sister to the Grand Menhir Brisé in Britanny, once the tallest prehistoric monolith in Europe. One purpose of the Grand Menhir seems to have been its use as a long range foresight for accurate observations of the Moon. Was the Obelisk perhaps used in the same way?

Part of the South Temple from the Central Obelisk 10 July 1723.

THE NORTH CIRCLE
looking west

Of the North Circle just four stones remain today. It is thought to have measured 340 feet across, the same as the South Circle, although some sources disagree, saying it was nearer 320 feet. At its centre a 'Cove' (*see next page*) of three huge stones once stood, two of which remain today.

There are actually still fallen and buried stones at Avebury as Alexander Keiller's restoration was interrupted by the war and never resumed. Maybe one day further stones will be put up again (surely a better use of our public money than horrible rusting metal sculptures overlooking motorways).

It is thought that there used to be twenty seven stones in the North Circle, with another three in the Cove, again making thirty in all. There may well have been an inner circle too, of twelve stones, 170 feet across (*see page 3*).

The fallen stone on which the gentleman leans to gaze westwards is still there. It is near the eastern entrance to Avebury, which is also nowadays the quietest and most attractive, the ancient route down from the Ridgeway. Look for the amazing beech trees which still guard the way.

THE COVE

a lunar clue at the centre of the north circle

Two of the most striking stones of the whole Avebury complex still stand at the centre of the northern circle. There used to be three in a cup shape, open to the north-east.

The Cove points to the spot over Hackpen Hill where the full moon rises at midwinter. The exact place indicated is called the northernmost moonrising. Full moons at midwinter follow roughly the same high passage and rising and setting places as the midsummer sun. The midsummer full moon accordingly behaves like the low midwinter sun.

Just west of Avebury the two stones known as Adam and Eve still stand in a field. They are all that is left of the Beckhampton Cove, beside the vanished avenue (*page 58*).

Coves are very rare, and all seem to have something to do with the Moon. One at Stanton Drew stone circles points, like Avebury's, to the northernmost moonrise; another at Arbor Low stone circle in Derbyshire points to the southernmost moonset. At the great stone circles in the northernmost Scottish isles, every nineteen years the midwinter full moon didn't even set in neolithic times!

The Cove of the Northern temple.

THE GEOMETRY OF AVEBURY
Professor Thom's breakthrough

Professor Alexander Thom, the foremost surveyor of stone circles to date, published this solution for the strange shape of Avebury in his book *Megalithic Sites in Britain* in 1967.

He noticed that the complex shape of the outer circle consists of seven separate curves and that four of these curves, shown here, have the *same* radius. All the measurements work out in easy multiples of megalithic yards (where one Megalithic yard = 2.72 feet), confirming his theory.

Especially interesting was his finding that three of these four centres of curvature lie in a precise 3-4-5 'Druids' triangle (shown opposite), here with sides 75, 100 and 125 MY. Professor Thom also measured the two inner circles both as 125 MY across, with 145 MY between their centres.

The triangular-shaped feature of small stones near the Obelisk in the south circle is still unexplained - ideas about it veer all over the place. It looks a bit like the triangle the whole of Avebury is based on.

The Outer Circle is thought to once have had 99 stones.

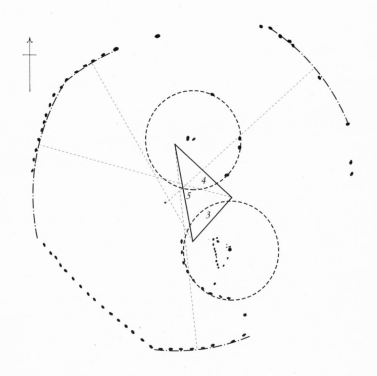

THE HEAVENLY SCIENCES
27, 29 and 99 stones

People often think of our ancestors as cavemen or prophets but they were also sophisticated astronomers. Robin Heath's recent work on Avebury shows just how clever they were.

Every eight years, Venus (our closest planet) draws an amazing fivefold flower shape round the Earth (*opposite below right*). But also, every eight years, there are almost exactly 99 full moons. The numbers are: 2921.9 days for eight years, 2920 days for the Venus cycle and 2923.5 days for 99 full moons. Perhaps the 99 stones of the outer circle each represent one Moon of the flowery eight-year Venus cycle.

But what about 27 and 29? Well, for a start, the Moon takes 27.3 days to return to any given star, and there are 29.5 days between full Moons! These are key lunar numbers. 27 and 29 stones also add up to 56, the number of Aubrey holes at Stonehenge, and the secret number for eclipse prediction.

The picture opposite shows Avebury's *precise* position one seventh of a circle up from the equator, and a peculiar relationship between Avebury and the Great Pyramid.

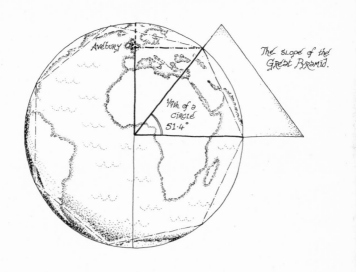

Avebury

¼th of a
CIRCLE
51·4°

The slope of the
Great Pyramid.

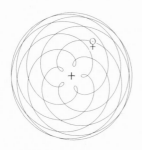

♀

+

Giza

30°

The slope of
Silbury Hill

AVEBURY'S CORNERS
hidden angles & passages

Few stone circles are circular but Avebury is most unusual in that it has two sharp corners! Why? The two tightest corners line up with the two centres of the inner circles to form two corridors. The narrow corridor points exactly to the top of Silbury Hill. From the summit of Silbury Hill midsummer sunrise and sunset divide the horizon into two sevenths of a circle. The extreme winter points do the same, leaving a total solar horizon zone of three sevenths of a circle.

If the inner radius of Avebury's inner circles is three, then the distance between their centres is seven. Three to seven. Avebury lies *exactly* three-sevenths of the way between the pole and the equator. A rectangle three wide and seven high also gives a diagonal which is an excellent value for the tilt of the earth, currently 23.4°.

The angle between the wide corridor and the line connecting the two circles is again a seventh of a circle, 51° 25' 42", the exact latitude of the very centre of Avebury.

Seven was an important number to our ancestors as they knew seven heavenly bodies and knew of seven metals.

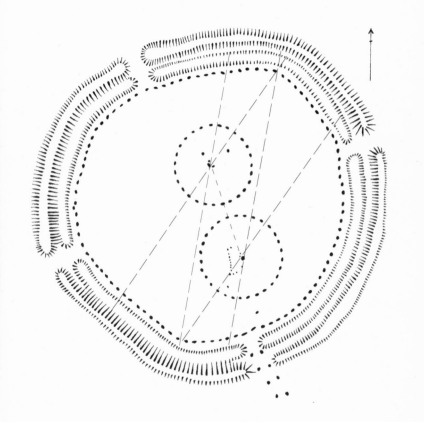

THE AVENUE
a serpent of stone

The Stone Avenue at Avebury is very fine. It connected the stone circles with the Sanctuary. Archaeologists believe the Avenue was built about four and a half thousand years ago, after the circles, then the ditch and the bank had been finished. Finally, when they had finished the Avenue, the builders replaced the hut at the Sanctuary with stone circles.

The Avebury Avenue had about one hundred pairs of facing

stones. Tall pillar-like stones (male) were chosen to face wider diamond or clover-leaf shaped ones (female). Research shows that people used to walk the outside of the Avenue.

Like much of Avebury the Avenue was restored in the late 1930's by Alexander Keiller. Stone row are quite rare in the British Isles and the most extensive in the world are at Carnac in France. The nearest to Avebury can be found at Stanton Drew stone circles, near Bristol. Merrivale in Dartmoor has lovely stone rows too.

THE SANCTUARY
at the end of the avenue

The Sanctuary lies at the end of the Avenue, alongside the Ridgeway path. Marker posts today show different constructions from four different dates of building activity. Archaeologists have noticed that the numbers of posts in each ring are almost always multiples of four.

A timber structure first stood here five thousand years ago, a few hundred years before Silbury Hill was started. A thousand years later, with Silbury, Avebury and the Avenue finished, stone circles were built here, either inside or replacing the hut. Stones still visible in the engraving were removed soon after Stukely's visit. Just one remains today.

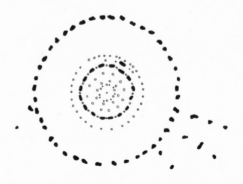

THE SERPENT'S HEAD
and other ideas

William Stukeley thought that the Sanctuary represented the head of a huge serpent, an idea supported by writer Michael Dames, who adds that the Sanctuary represented the Candlemas point in a landscape fertility cycle.

Renowned dowsers Hamish Miller and Paul Broadhurst found that the Sanctuary marks one of the crossing places of two enormous male and female earth energy currents which weave around the 'Michael line' (*see page 6*), other authorities hold that the Sanctuary is an arm of a huge pentagram set out in the landscape around Avebury, defining the positions of its elements. The fact is that we do not know it all and the truth may be stranger than we think.

It is quite possible that we will *never* know what it was like to be alive five thousand years ago; in the muddle of all of our incredible technological advances we may have lost some very simple perceptions which, if we regained them, might enable us to read Avebury, it's careful geometry, metrology, astronomy and landscaping, like a simple book.

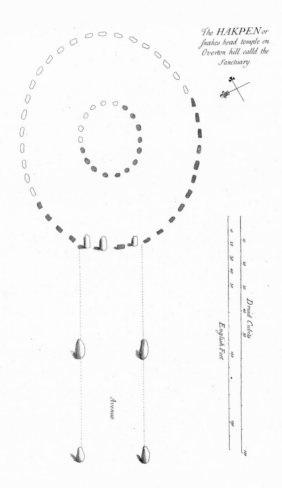

The *HAKPEN* or
fnakes head temple on
Overton hill. call'd the
Sanctuary

Druid Cubits

English Feet

Avenue

GLIMPSES OF ANOTHER AVENUE
the serpent's tail

There may have been a second avenue leading west from Avebury, then again there may have not. Recent research suggests that there was one.

William Stukeley was convinced of it and this is his engraving of its route from his book of 1743. To his great disapproval stones were being taken away while he was

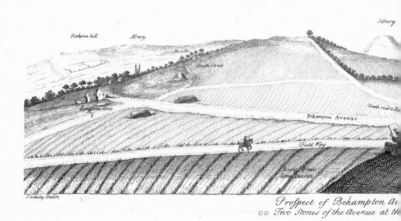

Profpect of Bekampton A
⊙⊙ Two Stones of the Avenue at the

writing and he shows the position of recently removed stones with a circle. Stukeley was fascinated with snakes and lost wisdom traditions. He encouraged other folk of the day to join him by founding the modern Druid orders.

Adam and Eve are the two remaining stones of Longstone Cove, a second cove to the one inside the stone circle, and are just visible on the left side of the picture. They are always well worth a visit *(see page 58).*

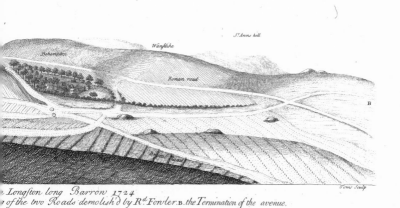

Longston long Barrow 1724
of the two Roads demolish'd by R^d Fowler. B. the Termination of the avenue.

SILBURY HILL
the eighth wonder of the world

South of Avebury, over Waden Hill, Silbury Hill rises from its boggy bed. It is the largest neolithic man-made mound in all of Europe. The silky grass exterior hides a stepped pyramid built of *seven* concentric drums. Inside are many layers of chalk, mossy soil and gravel. Hazel twigs found at Silbury's core suggest it is five thousand years old. Like the henge around Avebury it is thought to have once been without its grass-covering, simply shining white chalk.

In the last century a Yorkshireman, Moses B. Cotsworth, suggested that, like the Egyptian Pyramids, Silbury Hill could have been used as an accuarate calendar. A 95 foot pole on the top of the hill would have cast a midday shadow which would have touched the edge of the platform, the base of the hill and a stone (set in the field to the north of Silbury) at midsummer, equinox and midwinter respectively.

Silbury Hill has a little known sister. Known as Merlin's Mount, the huge tree-covered mound stands in the grounds of Marlborough College with a spiral path up it.

South of Silbury Hill is Swallowhead Spring.

STUKELEY'S GEOMETRY
what on earth were they up to?

Silbury Hill does fascinate people – it is our own Great Pyramid, built at the same time that the Egyptians were making theirs. We built our temples in Megalithic yards, and the Egyptians built theirs in Royal cubits; the difference between the two is *exactly* one (now illegal) British foot.

In Stukeley's picture the angle of slope is 40°, in other learned volumes the figure is given as 30°. Whatever the slope Silbury Hill is a steep climb and the track shown in Stukeley's picture is still there today. An iron horse bit, found in the Hill during the last century is also shown.

The top of Silbury Hill is just visible from Avebury. If you jump in the air at the stone circles you can see the top of Silbury Hill over Waden Hill, if you lie down you can't.

St. Anne's Hill is behind Silbury Hill to the south-west. Later known as Tan Hill it has long been the site of a summer fair and travelling people still make their way there today.

With a fire lit on Tan Hill, and dancers on Silbury Hill, mile-long shadows could be cast into Avebury.

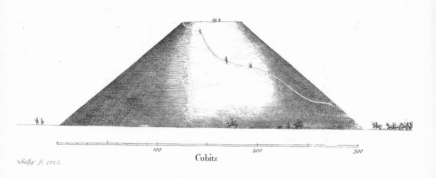

The Geometry of Silbury hill.

100   200   300

Cubits

Stukeley f. 1723.

45

HIDDEN CURRENTS
evidence of a lost science

_____

In 1969, Guy Underwood, a dowser from Bradford-on-Avon, published a book called *The Pattern of the Past*. In it he suggested that ancient peoples had been sensitive to subtle earth currents which he could detect using dowsing rods. He proposed that stone circles, burial mounds and, later, churches were sited at places where these currents converged.

In Underwood's top picture opposite we see a map of the the subtle lines of force at the beginning of the Avenue, where it connects with the stone circles. The lower picture shows his geodetic survey of Silbury Hill, complete with subtle energy lines, which he called 'aquastats'. In a very strange way the diagram captures something about the feeling of the place. Were our ancestors engineering the energy?

Dowsers are today used by water authorities, farmers and telephone companies to find water, pipes and cables. Archaeologists have even been known to use them to locate hidden or buried walls. Many dowsers are convinced that the dowsing art may once have been more widespread and natural, possibly forming part of an ancient science and perception, now almost gone.

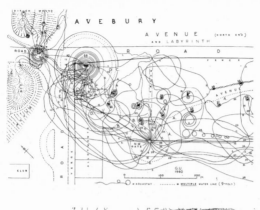

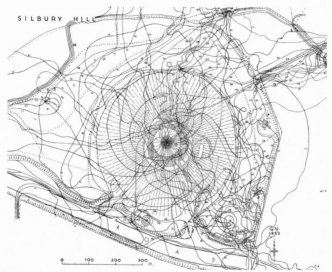

WEST KENNET
the longbarrow

This is not a very good picture of the longbarrow, but it will suffice. Nowadays you can go inside and poke around in the chambers. No-one really knows what longbarrows were built for. They appeared around the *start* of the great stone circle building period and often were built close to *cursuses*, huge mile-long runway-like things built by our ancestors all over the country, also for no known reason.

Some people think long-barrows were kingly burial chambers, because bones are found inside in small chambers off the main passageway, others think that they were early churches of some kind (we bury our Kings in churches too). Professor John North recently found that long-barrows are often precisely aligned on the rising of bright stars, something the Pyramids do as well. Today tourists wander in and out with flashing cameras, and hippies pollute them with paraffin candles and peculiar ideas.

Long barrows are almost always found on the edge of chalk deposits. They are best visited silently on frosty moonlit nights when they can emit a distinct blue flicker.

PAN'S DEN
the Avebury quoit

On the other side of Fyfield Down is a dolmen, close to the A4. Known as the *Devil's Den*, it consists of a capstone suspended on three uprights. I prefer *Pan's Den*.

Dolmens like this one were often covered with an earthen mound. It is not known if they were burial places, meditation chambers or neolithic follies. Another peculiar piece of the neolithic jigsaw puzzle!

Many ancient sites were given the D-name, the country-side is full of Devil's Stones; the Devil's Dyke and the Devil's Chair being other examples. It has been said that this all goes back to Bacchus, and the shaggy legs and goaty horns of Pan, the king of the faeries. Whether fairies really are dangerous or not nobody knows, but places (and people) with strong connections to the ancient earth traditions quickly suffered as understanding faded to be replaced by fear of the unknown. Despite centuries of repression, different levels of tradition nevertheless clung on in various remote parts of the British Isles, as they do in all truly ancient cultures, and you must walk through a field dedicated to St. Pesticide to get to the Devil's Den today.

MYSTERIOUS MOUNDS
barrows everywhere

Round Barrows litter the ancient landscape around Avebury. There are various kinds - Bowl Barrows, Bell Barrows, Disc Barrows, Pond Barrows, Saucer Barrows, Beam Barrows and many others. Along the Ridgeway they are found clustered together in groups and boast glorious stands of Beech trees, planted as a fad in Victorian times.

Barrows sometimes have skeletons in them. Sometimes they contain a circle of stones. On rare occasions they contain

buried treasure, and this has led to many a fruitless and destructive excavation over the centuries.

Some people think barrows represent constellations of stars, mapped down onto the earth, others suggest they are built where early crop circles appeared (some crop circles look very like neolithic rock carvings) or even where spaceships landed long long ago. In later times great warriors were buried in barrows, but most of the earlier ones are empty. Wilheim Reich thought they were part of the earth-energy grid, functioning a little like electrical condensers.

MORE MYSTERIES
lost artifacts and patterns of unicorns

———————————

Much has been lost. The dolmen (*opposite top*) and the magical barrow (*opposite below*) were both recorded by Stukeley in his book on Avebury. Both are no longer with us. Stukeley wrote of the Monkton Millbarrow:

"In Monkton, west of the town, is a large and flat long barrow ... 215f long 55 broad set round with great stones. It stands due east and west, the broadest end eastward. Its breadth the fourth part of its length: a most magificent sepulchre, and call'd Milbarrow."

Far away to the north-east on the Ridgeway path can be found the ancient Uffington White Horse hill figure (*below*), and another little Silbury Hill called Dragon Hill. Many other more modern White Horses cluster in the area and if you draw lines between them they cross at Avebury.

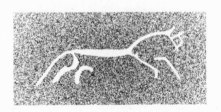

*In Monkton field
by Abury*

Abury

THE FUNCTION OF AVEBURY
the preservation of a fading cosmology

Across the world people are flocking to ancient temples. Why? Perhaps it is because they *do* something to us.

Scientists and glossy media people today tell us how to look at the world and advise us what to buy. A recent fashion is to employ sacred imagery to sell the profane. Meanwhile, as we are all told every day by the same people, the forests thin and the earth becomes hotter and drier and every fifty years there are twice as many of us on this tiny planet. This is all very important and we all know about it.

I believe Avebury was built to last - possibly by a culture which knew it needed to preserve something that they knew would be lost for some time. In Julian Jaynes' book *The Origin of Consciousness in the Breakdown of the Bicameral Mind* he suggests that these people may have experienced reality in such a different way to ourselves as to make all comparisons theoretical. Their science seems to have been so direct and precise that it would make our finest scientists today seem as blind men to them. I think these places may have been built as much for *our* time as for theirs by people more clairvoyant and star-born than we know.

Adam and Eve,
all that remain of the Beckhampton Avenue Cove.